Horse AND Pony
MAGAZINE

HORSE & PONY
CARE

Jackie Budd

RINGPRESS

Ringpress Books

Interpet Publishing, Vincent Lane, Dorking, Surrey, RH4 3YX, United Kingdom
First published 1996 in association with **Horse & Pony Magazine**

Reprinted 2002

© 1996 Ringpress Books Ltd. and Jackie Budd

ISBN 1 86054 071 6

Printed and bound in Singapore

All photographs courtesy of **Horse & Pony Magazine**.

CONTENTS

LIVING OUTDOORS is the most natural way of life for a pony. Most ponies, given a choice, would prefer to be out in the field where they can get plenty of fresh air, exercise, and free access to food in the company of their friends, than be confined to a stable. Even so, it is not a case of 'any field will do'. For a field-kept pony to stay happy and healthy his home must be safe and suitable to live in.

CHECK LIST

EVERY field must have a constant supply of clean, fresh water. Ideally, this will come from the mains to a trough. The trough should not have sharp corners or edges. Some fields may have a stream, but you can't be sure of clean water. Mucky ponds are danger to ponies and need fencing off. If there's no piped water, fill a large container, or buckets – but remember, ponies drink up to eight gallons (36 litres) a day!

IN the wild, ponies would always find a place to get out of the cold wind and rain, or take shade from flies and the hot sun. Make sure your field has somewhere like this. It could be natural shelter from a large tree or hedge, or best of all, a purpose-built shed. The shelter must be roomy enough for all the occupants to use, and it must have clean, dry bedding inside. Position the shed away from the prevailing wind on a high, well-drained spot.

MOST of the year your pony will be living off the grass beneath his feet, so the pasture must have reasonable feed value. Ponies do not want rich pasture as this can make them ill. However, the field should not be bare and sour, boggy or full of weeds. There must be plenty of space and grass for the number of ponies living there — a good guide is to allow at least one and a half acres (6000sq m) per pony — a little more if the grazing is poor quality.

Field Care Tips

PONIES are fussy grazers who tend to eat the tastiest grass and leave the rest. Good grass soon gets over-grazed and becomes sour, while the poorer patches and 'toilet' areas are left to get overgrown. To keep the field in good condition:
● **PICK up all the droppings at least once a week.**
● **DIVIDE the field into sections, so part of the pasture can be regularly rested.**
● **SEE if the field can be grazed for a while by other livestock such as sheep or cattle.**
● **ASK the field owner about 'topping' the long patches and fertilising and chain harrowing the pasture every so often.**

ALTHOUGH ponies can adapt to living by themselves, they are naturally sociable animals and would be very lonely kept on their own. Choose a field with space for at least one friend, preferably another horse or pony.

styles

- ✓ Good grazing
- ✓ Company
- ✓ Fencing
- ✓ Gate
- ✓ Water
- ✓ Shelter

Fencing - right and wrong ways

PONIES can be incredibly accident-prone, and they are also brilliant escape artists! Rickety, low or unsafe fencing is asking for trouble – a saggy barbed-wire fence could cause a very nasty injury. The best types of fencing are post and rail, or a thick hedge. Plain wire can be used, but it must be kept taut. Remember to check all around the fencing regularly. Repairs should be done straight away.

Above: WRONG. This could cause injury. Below: RIGHT: Secure wooden fencing.

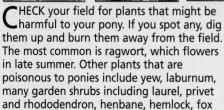

From left: Oak, ragwort, yew and dock

CHECK your field for plants that might be harmful to your pony. If you spot any, dig them up and burn them away from the field. The most common is ragwort, which flowers in late summer. Other plants that are poisonous to ponies include yew, laburnum, many garden shrubs including laurel, privet and rhododendron, henbane, hemlock, fox glove, horsetail, ground ivy, buttercups (in large amounts), and oak (mainly fallen acorns). Some weeds, such as nettles, docks and thistles, do no harm but show the pasture is poor. If your field is surrounded by houses, watch for gardeners throwing lawn clippings over the fence – these can give your pony stomach-ache.

YOUR field needs a sturdy, well-hung gate that is wide enough to lead your pony through safely, and has a secure fastening. Ponies tend to crowd around a gate and squabbles can develop, so gates are best positioned away from a corner and in a well-drained position. It is safest if the gate does not open on to a road.

Indoor Life

IN years gone by, horses were often tied up in stalls, so many could be kept in a small area.

Nowadays we give our horses the chance to move around in an individual 'loose-box', which could be in a yard or inside a large barn. Stables may be made of brick, stone, concrete blocks or strong timber, but they must be properly built or your pony's health could be affected.

Home, Sweet Home

MANY ponies can live out happily all year round in a good field with plenty of shelter, with extra feed in winter and, perhaps, the help of an outdoor rug in bad weather. Hardy, native types are well-equipped to cope with life outdoors. Other kinds of pony – particularly those that are part Thoroughbred or part Arab – have thinner skins and coats and do not cope well with cold, wet weather. During the winter months they will definitely need to wear rugs and to come inside to a warm stable at night.

However, horses were not designed to live indoors for long spells, and they do not like being kept in a stable all day, every day. Keeping a pony stabled full-time might make him easier to look after in some ways, because he will stay cleaner and be on-hand whenever you want to ride. But a fully stabled pony is a big responsibility as he relies on you for his every need. It is very time-consuming, as besides all your stable chores, you will have to put aside several hours every day to ride. Ponies confined for too long become bored and unhappy and can develop health and behaviour problems. It is a much better to use a combined system where your pony can be turned out in a field for daily exercise in winter, staying out all the time in summer.

Having a stable is useful even for field-kept ponies, in case your pony is ill or injured, or for bringing a greedy pony inside to restrict his grazing.

styles

Ventilation: Ponies need plenty of fresh air but dislike draughts. Every stable should have a window, protected or made of reinforced glass, preferably opening inwards at the top. There should be ventilation in the roof, too. Always leave the top door of a loose box open.

Space: The bigger the better is the rule! The minimum measurements would be 10ft x 10ft (3m x 3m) for a pony and 12ft x 12ft (3.75m x 3.75m) for a horse. The ceiling should be at least 10ft (3m) high.

Floor: Most stables have concrete floors. These are not ideal, but will do if they are sloped slightly to allow for drainage. The bedding must be kept clean.

Door: You want a sturdy door that is at least 4ft (1.25m) wide and 7½ft (2.2m) high, so the pony does not bang his head or sides going in and out.

Fittings: Avoid too many fittings as they only get in the way and might hurt your pony. There may be a manger, which should be around chest height and blocked in so the pony cannot get trapped underneath when he lies down. A hay rack should be at your pony's nose-height. Some stables have automatic waterers, but usually you would need to place a large bucket in one corner by the door. Light fittings and switches must be well out of reach. They should be the special covered type.

Types of livery

UNLESS you have a stable and field at home, you will be renting a stable and paying 'livery'. There are several systems you can choose from:

Grass livery: The cheapest way of keeping a pony, where you just rent a field. It is only suitable for the hardier kinds of pony.

DIY: Where you rent a stable and, preferably, the use of a field too. Quite cheap, but you need to look after all your pony's needs yourself.

Part livery: You pay a bit extra for the yard owner to do some tasks, like turning out and feeding. This is ideal because it lessens the work-load and there's always help and advice on hand.

Working livery: Where a pony is kept at a riding school, used and mainly cared for by the yard staff in return for a discounted charge.

Full livery: The pony is completely looked after and exercised by the yard staff, although you ride when you want Expensive – and you are missing half the fun!

Daily

DEPENDING on which way you keep your pony – whether he lives out or comes in at night, is on 'do it yourself' livery or you have some help – you will need to work out a daily routine.

You need to ensure he is well looked after, but also make sure the work fits in with school and when Mum or Dad can get you down to

Summer checklist

Morning AND evening:
● Catch your pony and check he is OK. Have a look to ensure there are no problems with the field. Make sure there is water in the trough.
● Pick out your pony's feet.
● Apply fly repellent if needed. Give a small feed, only if your pony is working hard.
● Bring your pony in for part of the day if his grazing needs to be restricted.

Once a week:
● Thoroughly check fencing.
● Pick up droppings.

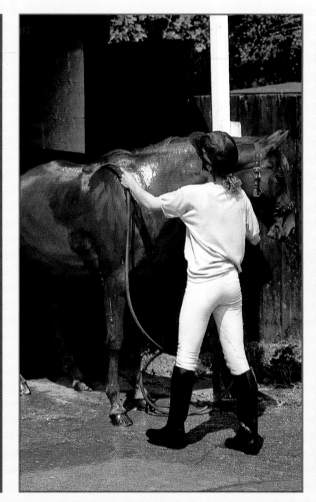

Summer TIPS

● **Flies** can make ponies thoroughly miserable in summer. Put on plenty of fly repellent, or bring your pony in to the shade of a stable or shelter in the hottest part of the day. A fly fringe can help.
● After a **sweaty** ride your pony will love a sponge or hose down. Be careful how you use a hose – he may be frightened of it at first.
● Don't **charge** about out riding when the ground is hard. It could make your pony lame.

Routines

the yard. Always try to stick to your timetable. Horses soon get to know when to expect a visit, so it is not only unkind but even harmful to keep changing the times you turn up each day. Your routine will be slightly different in summer and winter, as there are lots more jobs to be done in winter!

But all year round, whatever the weather and whether he lives in or out, your pony needs to be visited at least twice every day.

Here are the essential things you will need to do at each visit – apart from riding. You may need to arrange help from someone else – perhaps another pony-owning friend or the yard owner.

Winter checklist

Stabled at night
Morning: Ride first, if you have time. Give feed. Pick out feet. Put on an outdoor rug and turn your pony out in field. Muck out (this can be done in the evening if you wish). Fill hay net/rack. Clean and refill water buckets.
Evening: Muck out and do water and hay if not done before. Catch your pony. Give light grooming and pick out feet. Ride if you have time. Put on stable rug. Feed.
Once a week: Tidy muck-heap.
Field-kept
Morning AND evening: Catch your pony. Check the pony and the field. Pick out feet. Adjust the rug if one is worn, and replace it if it is very wet. Ride if you have time. Give feed and hay.
Once a week: Thoroughly check fencing. Pick up droppings.

Winter TIPS

● Never make your pony stand around getting cold. If he is clipped, leave a rug on until you are ready for a ride.
● If your pony is wet from sweating or from the rain when you come back from riding, you must not put a rug on him until his coat is dry or he could easily catch a chill. He will dry off more quickly if you fasten a 'string-vest' anti-sweat sheet underneath another light rug, or else wipe the pony over with a handful of straw or dry towels.
● Avoid washing your pony's body or legs too much in cold weather. Wait for mud to dry then gently brush it off.
● You can feed a field-kept pony using a bucket hung on the gate, but if his 'friends' are around this is sure to cause fights.

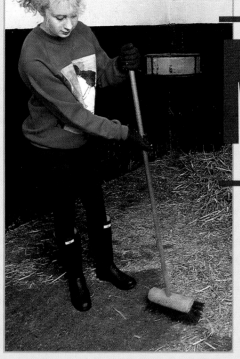

Mucking Out

WHENEVER your pony is in a stable he will need a deep, comfortable bed to keep him warm and to lay down on. It is true that ponies can doze standing up, but to have a really good rest they must lay down or stretch out flat. If the bed is too thin, a pony won't fancy lying down – and if he does, he may well risk knocks and scrapes.

STABLES must be mucked out every day. It is the job many pony owners hate, but with daily practice you will soon find it only takes a matter of minutes. It's not half as dirty and smelly as you would think – really!

A messy job, but it must be done...

1. Kit yourself out with the right tools: a large wheelbarrow, a stable fork, a shovel and a yard brush. For shavings or paper, use a shavings fork. A pair of rubber gloves can be handy to pick up scattered droppings.

2. Take the pony out of the stable – either turn him out or tie him up safely out of the way. Put the water buckets outside, too, and wheel in your barrow.

3. Use the fork, shovel or gloves to dig out the piles of droppings and put them into the barrow.

4. Now fork all the clean bedding into one pile, the slightly dirty stuff into another and the very dirty straight into the barrow.

5. Sweep the floor and corners clean and empty the barrow on the muck-heap.

6. Fork the remaining piles back into the centre. Add fresh bedding round the sides, shaking it out well. Make thick banks around the walls.

7. Once a week, leave the bed up for a while, disinfect the floor and allow it to dry.

WITH shavings and paper it is easier and more economical to pick up the droppings and worst wet patches daily and add some fresh bedding, and then have a thorough muck-out every one or two weeks.

'Deep' litter is a way of managing a bed where only the droppings are removed and new bedding piled on top. The whole bed is only cleared every few months. This sounds easy, but it can lead to foot problems, such as thrush, unless great care is taken. Ventilation must be good, or the air in the stable becomes stale and smelly.

& Bedding

THERE are several different types of bedding to choose from, each with its pros and cons. The most common are listed in the table, below. There are other kinds of pre-packaged bedding such as chopped hemp and dust-extracted straw. These are pricey, but good for ponies that cough on a straw bed.

Although shavings and paper cost more than straw, there is a lot in each bale. With care, you might only need to use one or two bales a week – you could easily go through five or six straw bales in the same time.

BEDDING	THE PROS	THE CONS
STRAW	Cheapest. Warm. Drains well. Easy to dispose of (rots down well for garden manure). Wheat straw is best – oat or barley straw is more likely to be eaten!	Some ponies are allergic to the dust and spores in straw, which causes coughing. Needs to be stored under cover. Makes a lot of muck.
WOOD SHAVINGS	Better for dust-sensitive ponies. Easy to muck out. Comes in plastic-wrapped bales so can be stored outside and bought as you need it.	Expensive. Takes ages to rot down, so could be hard to dispose of. Heavy to handle.
SHREDDED PAPER	Not as pricey as shavings. Warm. Rots faster than shavings but not as well as straw. Drains well. Dust-free. Can be stored outside and bought as needed.	Blows everywhere in the wind!

Tips

♦ Whatever bedding you use, put down plenty and spread it evenly. You should be able to stick the fork right in and not be able to touch the floor.

♦ The banks around the sides keep out draughts, protect against knocks if your pony should lie up against the wall, and help prevent him getting 'cast' – that is, lying down and finding he is wedged in and cannot get up again.

♦ A muck-heap attracts flies, so it should be sited well away from the stables. Try to keep it tidy, or it will soon be spreading in every direction!

♦ Some greedy ponies think their straw bed is there to be eaten. If you want to control nibbling, the only certain way is to change to a less tasty material!

Feeding:

FEEDING a pony correctly is one of the most important things an owner has to learn. It is a big subject, but not quite as complicated as it seems so long as you stick to a few basic rules.

The first thing to remember is that every pony is different and has his own feeding needs, so you must find out what is best for your pony – never just assume he will be fine eating what the horse next-door has.

The other point to bear in mind is that ponies' insides are quite different to those of other animals, such as ourselves. Ponies have amazingly intricate and delicate digestive systems that are easily upset, leading to problems like colic (horsey stomach-ache) that can be very serious. Lots of difficulties can come from being careless about feeding, but learn and stick to the *'Golden Rules of Feeding'* and you will not go far wrong.

1 Little and often

Nature designed horses and ponies to eat grass, taking in a little food at a time, almost all day long. They have small stomachs (about the size of a rugby ball) that cannot cope with big meals. A large quantity of food cannot be digested properly and could easily cause a blockage. Therefore, make sure that hay or grass is always available, and split 'concentrate' feeds into several small meals a day. *Do not give more than 1kg (2lbs) in one feed to a small pony or 1.5kg (3lbs) to a larger pony.*

2 Feed at regular times

Ponies like routine – and so do their stomachs! Stick to frequent, regular meal-times that your pony will look forward to. Try not to dish up a large amount in one meal followed by a long period with no feed at all.

4 Plenty of fibre

Fibre means 'roughage' or 'bulk forage' – food like grass, hay or chaff. It is what the horse's digestion is designed to live on. Without plenty of fibre trickling through the system, it cannot work properly. So, especially if your pony is stabled a lot, give him plenty of hay and high-fibre feeds like chaff and sugar beet.

3 Water supply

A pony will drink up to eight gallons a day and needs water to digest his food. But, remember, his stomach is small – so have water on-hand all the time, or make sure he has had the chance to drink before a meal. Otherwise he might slurp it down and wash food out of his stomach before it has been digested. Or the water could make dry food swell painfully in the digestive system, which could cause a blockage.

5 Beware sudden changes

Ponies' insides are full of tiny microbes which help to break down and digest food. There is a unique microbe for every kind of food! That is why any alterations in the amount or kind of food you give have to be made gradually, to give the digestive system time to adjust.

6 Feed the best quality

Do not buy very cheap, poor-quality feed, or keep feedstuffs for too long or in damp or dusty conditions. Ponies cannot thrive on bad or musty food – it can actually make them ill. Feed the best you can afford and store it properly in airtight, vermin-proof containers to keep it fresh.

Golden Rules

7 Keep all your utensils clean

Would you fancy eating lunch off a plate no one had washed up since yesterday's supper? Then don't expect your pony to enjoy his meal and stay healthy if he has to eat out of a grimy, grubby bucket or manger. Cleaning utensils every day only takes a few minutes.

8 Wait at least an hour before exercise

The horse's ancestors needed to be able to gallop away from predators at speed, so they developed large lungs and small stomachs. Lying just behind the lungs, a full stomach can make it hard for a pony to breathe easily. Anyway, would you be comfy working out straight after dinner?

9 Feed something succulent

Juicy grass is ponies' favourite food, and the best thing for them (as long as they don't overdo it!). But they appreciate succulent extras added to their feed. Apples, carrots, root vegetables and sugar beet shreds or nuts are all enjoyable for ponies, especially those that don't get out into the field very often.

10 Feed as an individual

This is back where we started – learning that every pony has his own requirements when it comes to planning the amount and type of food he eats. His size, build, age, workload, character, the weather, and how he is kept, are among the things you must consider.

NO WAY BACK!

PART of a pony's problem with feeding is that he cannot be sick, so once he has swallowed a mouthful, it's in – for better or worse! The food then has to travel through over 30 metres of intestines, taking up to three days, before it passes out of the other end. So, you can imagine that if he takes in something harmful, a lot of damage can be done.

Feeding:

KNOWING how to feed is only part of the feeding game. Now you need to swot up on what your pony needs to eat if you want to keep him healthy and able to do his best for you. In just the same way that we are all supposed to eat a balanced, nutritious diet to keep us in trim, ponies also need to get the right kind of food that contains a balance of all the nutrients they need.

A PONY NEEDS . . .

Carbohydrates: To provide energy to stay alive and do extra work like being ridden

Protein: To build up cells and bones, and to help him grow and repair himself after illness or injury.

Fibre: To keep his digestion working properly.

Fats: To keep him warm and provide extra energy if needed.

Vitamins and minerals: To keep the body healthy.

Different kinds of food contain different levels of nutrients, so it will not do just to feed anything and hope for the best. For example, you might find you are feeding a high carbohydrate diet that makes him so full of energy that you have trouble staying on!

Types of fibre

IN the wild, grass provides a pony with all the nutrients he needs. When one area has been grazed down, the herd moves on to a fresh, juicier place. The trouble for ponies these days is that we coop them up in small fields and stables, and expect them to charge about with us on their backs. Though a well-managed pasture will provide enough nourishment for this in spring and summer, by autumn there is no goodness left. We have to replace that nourishment by providing grass in dried form – hay. Grass and hay are the main sources of the bulk and fibre essential to a horse's diet.

Grass The best and most natural food for your pony. Good-quality grass will provide a complete balanced diet during the spring and summer. When grass is poor – in winter, during a very dry summer or if the field is over-grazed – hay must be fed.

The two parts to every pony's diet

BESIDES water, a pony's diet is made up of either just one kind of food – bulk feed such as grass and hay, or two kinds of food – bulk fibre foods plus concentrate foods such as nuts, mixes, or grains like oats or barley. Bulk is the most important because a pony cannot survive without this fibre in his diet. He can live without concentrates, although they provide very useful extra energy he needs for work and for warmth.

Hay This is grass cut and dried in early summer when it is at its best, and stored to feed to horses in winter or when they are stabled. Only feed hay that is crisp, sweet-smelling and contains a good mixture of nutritious grasses. Poor hay that is dusty, mouldy, yellow or full of weeds is bad for ponies. There are two types – seed hay that has been grown specially, and meadow hay which is softer and finer and has been cut off ordinary pasture. Hay can be fed from a rack or from a haynet. If you use a net, tie it high so when it hangs empty there is no risk of a pony's foot getting caught.

Fibre

Chaff

Usually straw, or a mix of hay and straw, that has been chopped up and is often covered with molasses. You can also buy alfalfa chaff which is a very nutritious clover-like plant, high in calcium. A good way of adding fibre to the diet.

If you use a haynet, always tie it high up in the stable.

Haylage

Hay that has been treated and sealed into bags when it is half-dry. It is totally dust-free, so is good for ponies sensitive to dust and spores in ordinary hay. It is a good alternative to hay, but it is very rich so it must be fed sparingly.

TIP

SUCCULENT foods like apples, carrots, root crops and sugar beet also have a high fibre content. Always chop lengthways to avoid the risk of choking, and do not over-feed or you may give your pony diarrhoea!

1

2

BULK forage by itself can keep a pony ticking along fine, but it doesn't contain much energy. In winter, most of what it does have is used up just keeping the pony warm. So whenever a pony is being ridden regularly or the weather is bad, he will probably need to be given extra meals of concentrate or 'hard feed'.

Some ponies, especially hardy cob or native types, need very little or no concentrate feed because they are such 'good doers' – that is, they thrive on relatively little feed. Other ponies tend to lose weight or feel the cold unless they are given plenty of concentrates on top of their hay and grass.

Whatever concentrates are fed, the balance of nutrients in them must be just right. So it is important to know something about the different types of feedstuffs, particularly if you plan to mix several sorts. That is why 'compound feeds' like nuts or coarse mixes are so brilliant, because the manufacturer has done all of the hard work for you, taking all the worry and effort out of making up a diet for your pony. It also means that you do not have to store lots of bags of feed, which always seem to run out at different times!

Feeding:

Choices on the Menu...

Nuts/cubes

● A balanced mixture of traditional feedstuffs crushed and pressed into pellets.

● Far and away the best (and most economical) hard feed for almost all riding ponies and horses. Together with water and hay/grass, it contains all your pony needs.

● **Watch out!** There is no need to add anything else to a diet of nuts except chaff and apples/carrots, or you will upset the formula.

● Buy the right type of nut, as there are varieties to suit many different needs. There are low-energy nuts for ponies doing little work, and special nuts for competition horses, brood mares and youngsters.

Q & A

QUESTION: Does my pony need a vitamin or mineral supplement?
ANSWER: If he's in good health and getting a balanced diet the answer is most probably 'No'. Growing or hard-working ponies might need extra, or your vet might advise a supplement to help with special problems like cracked feet.

Hard Feeds

Varieties of hard feed:
(from left):

1 Nuts
2 Coarse mix
3 Rolled oats
4 Flaked barley
5 Flaked maize

Choices on the Menu...   Choices on the Menu...

Coarse mix

● A ready-formulated mix like nuts, but bought in muesli form.

● Great for pony owners, for the same reasons as nuts.

● **Watch out!** (*See Nuts*).

Oats

● Bought crushed, rolled or bruised so they are easily digested.

● For ponies doing a lot of work.

● **Watch out!** Guaranteed to 'fizz' up the doziest pony. They must be fed with a calcium-rich food to maintain the right balance of two important minerals, calcium and phosphorous.

Barley

● Bought flaked, micronised or extruded (forms of cooking). Whole barley can be boiled into a mash.

● Gives energy to ponies in regular work. Good for putting on weight and for warmth.

● **Watch out!** Can hot up some ponies. Should not make up more than a third of the total ration.

Flaked maize

● Used for hard-working ponies, in small amounts. Helps put on condition.

● **Watch out!** High in energy and also phosphorous (see Oats). Feed sparingly.

Broad bran

● Traditionally given as a mash for resting, sick or old horses, as when prepared in this way it works as a laxative.

● **Watch out!** Besides being expensive, it can cause calcium deficiency. Adding chaff to the feed is a better source of fibre.

Dried sugar beet

● Comes as shreds or pellets, with added molasses.

● Good for adding fibre to hard feeds. High in energy and calcium. Tasty.

● **Watch out!** Must be soaked in water for at least 12 hours before feeding, because it swells amazingly. Do not keep soaked beet for more than 48 hours or it starts to ferment. Don't confuse beet nuts with similar-looking ordinary pony nuts.

Minerals, Vitamins

The only essential mineral you will need to add to your pony's diet is a teaspoonful of salt. Add to the feed daily or put a salt lick on the stable wall.

Feeding:

HALF of the secret of feeding is knowing how much to give. It takes experience to judge whether your pony is looking too fat and so needs less food, too thin and so needs more, or is in exactly the right condition. As a rough guide, if you can feel his ribs when you press your fingers on his sides he is about right. If his ribs can be seen, he's looking poor.

If you can't feel a hint of ribs in there, he's way too fat! Being fat isn't a sign of a health – a fat pony is at risk from serious diseases such as laminitis.

In summer few ponies need extra food on top of the grass in their field. In fact, many do so well on spring and summer grass that they may need their grazing limited by being brought in for part of the day, or the paddock may have to be divided up to stop them getting over-weight.

If dry weather frazzles the grass it may be necessary to give some hay, but only hard-working ponies are likely to need any concentrate feed in summer.   In winter, you will need to keep a close eye on your pony's condition to decide whether he needs hard feed on top of his hay to maintain his weight and energy for the work you plan to do. Follow the steps on pages 20-21 to plan a personal autumn and winter diet plan for your pony.

Native pony

13hh
Bodyweight: 250kg.
Lives: Out all year.
Work: Daily ride in summer, weekends only in winter.
Daily diet: Summer – grass only. Winter – 6kg hay; 1-1.5kg pony nuts or low energy mix, if necessary, plus a handful of chaff and carrots.

Diets

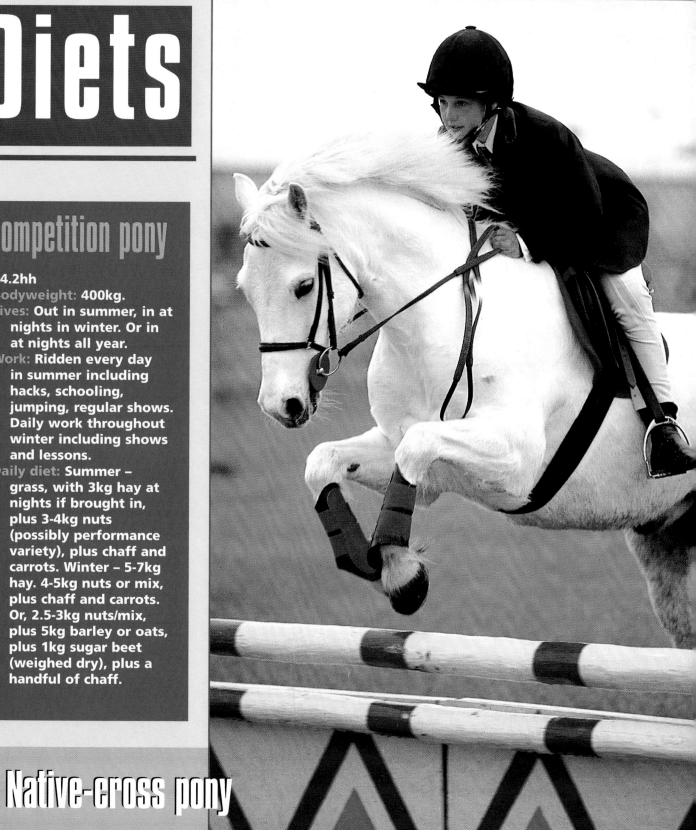

Competition pony

14.2hh
Bodyweight: 400kg.
Lives: Out in summer, in at nights in winter. Or in at nights all year.
Work: Ridden every day in summer including hacks, schooling, jumping, regular shows. Daily work throughout winter including shows and lessons.
Daily diet: Summer – grass, with 3kg hay at nights if brought in, plus 3-4kg nuts (possibly performance variety), plus chaff and carrots. Winter – 5-7kg hay. 4-5kg nuts or mix, plus chaff and carrots. Or, 2.5-3kg nuts/mix, plus 5kg barley or oats, plus 1kg sugar beet (weighed dry), plus a handful of chaff.

Native-cross pony

14hh
Bodyweight: 350kg.
Lives: Out in summer; in at nights in winter.
Work: Daily rides plus some shows/rallies. In winter, two or three week-day rides plus occasional lesson/rally.
Daily diet: Summer – grass, with 2-2.5kg nuts or low-energy mix, only if necessary. Winter – 6-7kg hay. 2.5-3.5kg nuts or low-energy mix, plus a handful chaff and carrots.

Feeding:

1 Basic amount

The basic amount of food a pony needs each day is worked out according to his bodyweight. He will require approximately 1kg of food a day per 500kg bodyweight. There is a simple calculation you can do to estimate his bodyweight in kg (though you may need your calculator or mum and dad's help to work it out!

Girth measurement in cm (squared) x length from chest to tail in cm divided by 8717.

2 How much bulk/fibre and concentrate?

How much of this total should be made up of hay/grass and how much of hard feed? Basically, the more work a pony is doing the greater proportion can be made up of hard feed (see panel below). But never give less than 50 per cent of the total as bulk.

3 What sort of concentrate?

Choose hard feed that suits your pony and his lifestyle to make up this part of his ration (see panel, below left).

Bulk v Concentrate

	grass/hay	concentrate
No work or occasional or weekend rides	100%	none, unless weather poor or grass scarce
Regular rides/lessons	70-80%	20-30%
Daily long or fast rides/lessons/shows	60%	40%

Feed v Lifestyle

General riding	Non-heating nuts or low energy coarse mix, perhaps with a handful of chaff and apples/carrots added
Ponies with special needs	Hard-working – try performance mix/nuts, or make up a ration including some barley/oats and sugar beet
	Lose weight easily or feel the cold – try including barley and sugar beet
	Old ponies – include sugar beet, boiled barley and alfalfa chaff

DO not just guess at weights. Check the weight of a scoopful of each kind of feed you are using (picture, right). Weigh hay by hooking a haynet to spring-scales, which you can buy cheaply from any feed merchant or tack shop.

Quantities

4 When might my pony need less feed?

Remember, you have to be flexible about feeding and use your common sense about your pony's condition. If any of the points below apply, he may not need quite as much food as the total you have calculated.

● In the spring and summer, especially when the grass starts growing.
● If he is a very 'good doer' or prone to laminitis. Many ponies get fat easily and do well on relatively little food.
● If he is getting too lively to ride or handle he may be getting too much or the wrong sort of food. Reduce the amount of concentrates he is getting and increase the hay/grass.
● If he has a live-wire temperament he may need very little hard feed. In both these cases, give only low-energy nuts or a high-fibre mix.

5 When should I increase the amount I feed my pony?

The quantity you feed may need to be increased:

● If the pony is not doing well on what he is getting, he looks thin or has no energy. Look at his teeth and check if he needs worming. Now increase his hay and time in the field, then his hard feed.
● Any time when the grass is poor or scarce.
● During bad weather, particularly if he lives out or is clipped.
● When your pony is working hard – such as during school holidays.
● In-foal mares, youngsters and oldies, who don't process their food as efficiently, have their own special needs. Discuss these with your vet.

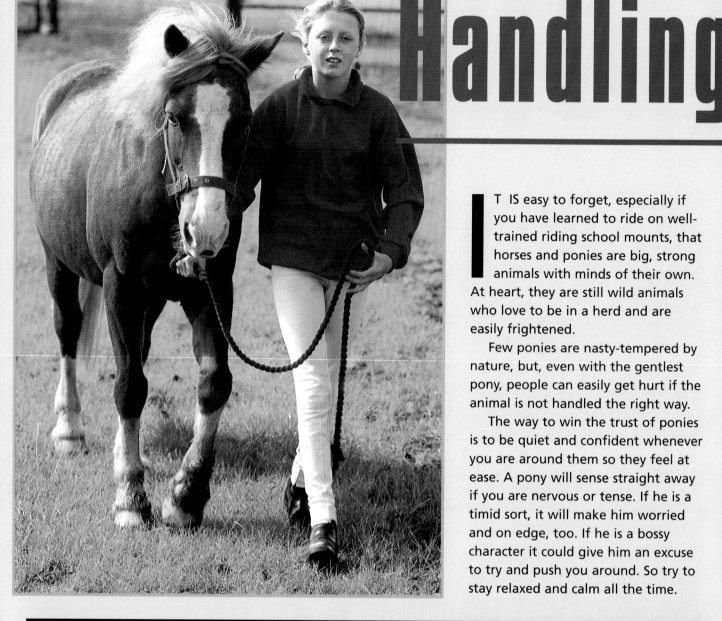

Handling

I T IS easy to forget, especially if you have learned to ride on well-trained riding school mounts, that horses and ponies are big, strong animals with minds of their own. At heart, they are still wild animals who love to be in a herd and are easily frightened.

Few ponies are nasty-tempered by nature, but, even with the gentlest pony, people can easily get hurt if the animal is not handled the right way.

The way to win the trust of ponies is to be quiet and confident whenever you are around them so they feel at ease. A pony will sense straight away if you are nervous or tense. If he is a timid sort, it will make him worried and on edge, too. If he is a bossy character it could give him an excuse to try and push you around. So try to stay relaxed and calm all the time.

LEADING A PONY SAFELY

LEADING is one of the most basic handling skills you need to learn to do safely, as it is easy to get trodden on, to get taken for a walk by the pony – or even to lose him altogether. Ponies are a lot stronger than we are, so the trick is not to let them realise this!

● Though a pony should get used to being led from either side, it is usual to lead from his left (near) side. If you ever have to lead a pony on the road, always place yourself between him and the on-coming traffic though, and use a bridle rather than a headcollar.

● Hold the lead rope about 25cm away from the pony's chin, with your right hand (left hand if you are leading from the right-hand side). Allow a little more rope to give him more freedom for his head if you are trotting. Hold the rest of the rope in your other hand keeping it off the ground.

● Walk right alongside the pony's head. Do not drag him along behind you or let him charge off in front.

● Do not hold on to the rope too tight or too close to his head – ponies hate feeling pressure or restriction on their heads and might panic.

● Never wrap the lead-rope around your hand or wrist. If the pony takes fright, you could be dragged along.

● If you want to turn the pony, for a vet or in the show ring, always turn him away from you, to avoid getting your toes squashed and give a clear view of his movement.

● If you are leading a tacked-up pony, make sure the stirrup irons are run up, not dangling. Take the reins over the pony's head. If he wears a running martingale, unbuckle the reins and unthread it, tie it in a loose knot and hold the reins over the head.

Approaching a pony

ALWAYS speak to a pony when you approach or handle him so he knows where you are. Never move suddenly or make loud, unexpected noises. Ponies cannot see behind them or very well in front of them, so walk steadily up to the pony's shoulder to let him see you, and stroke him firmly on the neck. Ponies love to be touched and scratched, as it is their own way of greeting each other. If you want to offer a titbit, make this an occasional treat rather than something your pony demands every time you appear. Hold your hand out flat so no fingers are mistaken for juicy pieces of carrot!

Speaking to your pony can help him understand what you want him to do. Make commands definite – such as, 'Over', or 'Walk on'. Praise him in a kind, soft voice, and if he needs telling off make it a stern, sharp 'No!' Both should come straight away, not when he has forgotten what he did. Always be fair and consistent in the way you treat and handle ponies so they know what is right and wrong behaviour.

LEFT: WRONG! Always hold your hand out flat when feeding a pony.

BEING tied up for grooming, mucking out or shoeing, for example, is one of the first lessons a young pony learns. But there is always a danger that something might startle even the quietest pony when he is tethered, which is when accidents can happen.

❖ Never leave a pony tied up alone.

❖ Leave plenty of space in between ponies tied up next to each other, especially if they are eating.

❖ Do not make the rope so short your pony can hardly move his head, or so long he could put a foot over it and get caught up.

❖ Never tie up using your reins – one tug and you have a broken bridle. Always put a headcollar on over your bridle and use the proper lead rope.

❖ Never tie your pony to a moveable object such as an open gate.

❖ Always attach your pony to something easily breakable in case disaster strikes, such as a loop of string tied to a fixed post or rail.

❖ Use a secure knot that your pony cannot undo, but you can – in a hurry if needs be. Practise your quick-release knot and use it!

Tying a quick-release knot

1. Push a loop of lead rope through your string. Twist the loop several times.
2. Make another loop of the free end of the rope and push it through the twisted loop.
3. To tighten, pull on the end of the rope attached to the headcollar.
4. The knot can be completely released by pulling on the free end of the rope.

Handling

AS MOST ponies live outdoors for most of the year, or are at least turned out often, knowing how to move around among loose ponies, to turn out and to catch a pony, is a big part of being pony-smart.

Ponies kept out together soon start to behave like a mini 'herd'. Anything out of the ordinary can make them excited or wary, such as a new arrival, activity nearby or even stormy weather.

You will notice that there are bossy characters and shy ones, and sometimes you may see them rearing up or kicking out in the field. They rarely mean to hurt each other at these times.

Usually the bad-tempered faces, laid-back ears and lifted heels are just a warning to the others to 'Watch out!'. But this natural behaviour does mean that we humans have to watch out too when we are in a field full of ponies, so as not to be caught in the firing line. A shod hoof can give a nasty kick.

Turning out

SWINGING open the gate and letting a pony go with a slap on the bottom is asking for trouble. Teach your pony to be well-mannered and to stay safe by:

■ Always opening the gate wide enough to pass through, but keeping hold of it as you go.

■ Leading the pony through, shutting the gate properly behind you – or the rest of the field occupants could disappear!

■ Walking a little way in and turning your pony around to face the gate. Make him stand quietly for a few moments before slipping his headcollar off carefully.

■ Never release him facing into the field – he could be over the horizon with you still attached!

Awkward customers...

SOME ponies are not that easy to get your hands on! Maybe the spring grass is too tasty, or they don't like the idea of work. Ask yourself why first, and, make sure your pony always associates being caught with pleasant experiences. Faced with a determined escape artist, here are some tips:

● Never grab at your pony or lose your temper. Do not try cornering or chasing him – he's quicker than you and you will be worn out long before he is!

Catching a pony

☐ **Walk into the field steadily and confidently, speaking so the ponies have time to see and hear you. Hold the headcollar neatly by your side.**

☐ **By all means have a treat in your pocket to reward your pony for being caught, but it is a bad idea to take a bucket into a field full of ponies. Before you know it, you will be in the middle of a riot!**

☐ **Approach at an angle to your pony's shoulder. With a friendly word and pat on the neck, slip the lead-rope around his neck. Put the headcollar round his nose, do up the headstrap securely and walk him quietly towards the gate.**

☐ **Even if your pony is standing by the gate, never try to lean over and put the headcollar on over the gate. Do not be lazy and take risks with ponies.**

● Be patient and give yourself plenty of time. Be prepared to make lots of visits just to catch him, feed and fuss him until he starts to change his mind about being caught.

● When you do get hold of him always reward him and never scold or he definitely won't come next time.

● Persistent offenders can be turned out in a well-fitting leather headcollar with a short length (about 25cm) of rope attached.

● Tactics for catching awkward customers include fencing off a small corner of the field to lure your pony into, walking round him in ever-decreasing circles, walking after him until he gives up moving away, or sitting down, waiting for his curiosity to overcome his reluctance to be caught!

Grooming:

GROOMING a pony obviously makes him look smarter, but a much more important reason for grooming is to keep the skin and coat healthy and clean. Different ponies will have different grooming routines according to what kind of lifestyle they lead.

Ponies who are stabled a lot need a thorough groom every day to help clean their skin and keep their coat in top condition. They can have a quick brush-over before exercise, called quartering, then a full groom afterwards, known as 'strapping'.

By putting lots of effort into your brushing, you can even improve the pony's circulation and muscle tone. If your pony lives out he will not thank you for going over the top with your grooming, because he needs to keep plenty of grease and oil in his coat for warmth and water-proofing, especially during winter. Field-kept ponies still need to be brushed over before a ride though, and will appreciate being kept comfortable and tidy.

Grooming is a perfect way to get to know a pony well. Though some ponies are particularly ticklish, most love being groomed. It must feel rather like a relaxing massage to them. It's also a perfect chance for you to look your pony over regularly for minor cuts and injuries, and to keep an eye on his general condition.

for health

TIP

DON'T forget, your kit will need cleaning regularly too, or it will be putting more dirt on your pony than it takes off!

The Kit

EVEN if you don't own your own pony, collecting a grooming kit means you'll be better prepared to help out at the stables. You will need in your box:

1 Dandy brush: A large brush with long, stiff bristles for taking off mud, dirt and dry sweat. Too hard to use on the head, mane or tail.

2 Body brush: A softer brush with shorter, denser bristles that cleans deep down into the coat.

3 Hoof pick: Removes bedding, mud or stones.

4 Hoof oil: Brushed on to the feet for smartness.

5 Rubber curry comb and plastic curry comb: Both great for getting dry mud off or removing loose hairs during Spring-time moulting.

6 Metal curry comb: Never use on the pony's body. Scrape it across the body brush to remove hairs, dust and scurf.

7 Water brush: Like a dandy brush with shorter, softer bristles. Used to scrub hooves and damp down the mane and top of the tail so they lie flat.

8 Sponges For bathing and freshening up the eyes, nostrils and dock areas.

9 Stable rubber: A cloth used to give an extra polish to the coat or dry damp areas.

10 Mane comb: For final combing through of mane and plaiting.

Grooming:

TIP

THOUGH mud, grass or stable stains might need to be wiped off, only brush when your pony's coat is dry. Brushing wet hair will not remove dirt, but it will scratch and chafe the skin.

If your pony is wet from the rain and you want to ride, scrape off as much wet as you can using the sweat scraper, then rub the saddle area with a towel. Do not put the saddle on until the coat has had a chance to dry properly.

After a day in the field

● Use the hoof pick twice daily to clear mud and stones from the feet. (See Picking out feet).

● Carefully sponge the eyes, nose and dock, using separate sponges for each. When cleaning eyes, wipe from back to front so dirt is not spread across the eye.

● If you are going for a ride, smarten up your pony by using the rubber curry comb to get off the worst of the mud.

● Now take the dandy brush and use it to-and-fro across the body, especially over the areas where the tack goes. Dirt left on here can soon cause sores. Around the head, it is best to use your fingers to pick off dry mud and then the softer body brush.

● A quick flick over with a body brush will not do any harm once in a while, but not every day. Tease out real tangles from the mane and tail with the fingers before finishing off with the body brush.

Routines

TIP

SOME awkward ponies will not pick their feet up immediately when you ask. If this happens, stay close to the leg and lean slightly into the pony's side, nudging him with your shoulder or elbow until he shifts his weight and gives you the chance to lift his foot. Do not lift a foot up too high, as this is very uncomfortable for a pony.

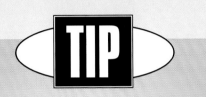

Picking out feet

TO PICK up and clean out the feet, take your hoof pick and stand alongside the pony's shoulder, facing his tail. Stroke his shoulder firmly, then run your hand down the back of the leg and when you reach the fetlock, gently tug the hair and say "Up".

Hold the front of the hoof with your fingers, using the hoof pick in your outside hand to scrape from the heels towards the toe. Always work in this direction, as it avoids hurting the sensitive frog (the V-shaped part of the sole) by mistake.

For the hind legs, stand close alongside the pony's quarters. Stroke him firmly and talk to him. Run your hand down the inside of the leg past the hock to the fetlock. Hold the fetlock around the back and ask the pony to lift it as before. Again, hold the foot with your fingers so the pony does not lean on you.

When you have finished cleaning the foot, don't just drop it. Put it down properly, or you could accidentally get kicked as the pony waves his foot about.

Grooming

F THE pony you ride spends a lot of time in the stable, you can go to town on the grooming because it really will help him to feel more comfortable. It is best to groom thoroughly after a ride, because this is when his skin will be warm. Another time when you might want to give your pony a really good brush-up is if you are going to a show – and it will not hurt field-kept ponies to have this done every once in a while.

Complete routine

● Tie up your pony and pick out each foot in turn. *(See Picking out feet)*.
● Brush off any dry dirt and sweat marks with the dandy brush or rubber curry comb. Start at the top of the neck and work down the body and legs.

● Tease out the mane with the fingers then work through it with the body brush. Now do the same with the tail.
● Starting near the head, groom the body with the body brush. Use firm, circular strokes, putting all your weight behind each one and always brushing in the direction of the hair. Every few strokes, scrape the brush across the metal curry comb to clean it. Clean the curry comb by tapping it on the floor.
● Undo the head collar, and, if the door is shut, remove it so you can gently brush the head with the body brush. If you are outside, keep the rope held around the pony's neck. Do the headcollar up again as soon as you have finished.
● Sponge the eyes, nose and dock *(see previous page)*.
● You can 'lay' the mane to keep it flat using a damp water brush.

ALWAYS use a brush in the hand nearest the pony's head. So when grooming the near (left) side use your left hand, and on the off (right) side use your right hand.

● Use the water brush to wash any mud off the feet. When they are dry, brush on some hoof oil to the outside for a finishing touch.

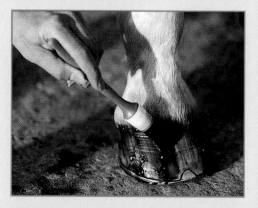

● Wipe the whole body over with the slightly-damp stable rubber for a final gloss and dust-over.

& Bathing

ON HOT summer days, or for that special occasion when your pony needs to be super-smart, a bath will be beneficial – it will do his coat good, and will help to keep flies at bay. You can wash the tail more often and during winter, but for a full bath stick to mild weather or chills are easily caught.

Bath time tips

● Many ponies dislike water, or may not be used to being bathed. Make sure a helper is available to hold the pony while you carefully introduce him to it.

● Never slosh the water about unnecessarily. Be especially careful if you are using a hose-pipe as this can be frightening to a pony.

● Use luke-warm water, except on the hottest days. Ponies no more like a cold shower than you do!

● Always use a proper horse shampoo. Many ponies have very sensitive skins.

● Dampen the coat and mane with the sponge or hose, then apply the shampoo (not too much!). Rub in gently. Now rinse off thoroughly, changing the water as you need to or using the hose.

● Use the sweat scraper to wipe off excess water.

The hard edge is for the body and the flexible edge for the legs.

● Take care not to get shampoo in your pony's eyes.

● When washing the tail, stand slightly to one side. Soak it, then apply a little shampoo and rub in. Rinse it out thoroughly, squeeze out most of the water and swing the tail around gently to help it dry.

● Use a towel to dry the heels well.

● Walk the pony around until he is dry, then go over with the body brush. A sweat rug, with a light cotton sheet on top, will let him dry without getting cold if there is a chill in the air.

● Remember, if you let your pony loose in the field with a damp coat, he is sure to roll in the dust!

Trimming

THERE are several places you can take the scissors to, in order to make your pony look that bit tidier. On the whole, it is best not to go too mad with the trimming on a field-kept pony, especially in winter, as he grows all that hair for a very good reason. But a bit of trimming will smarten him up no end and not do any harm.

Whiskers: Kind, caring owners never trim off a pony's whiskers. It would be unfair, as he uses them all the time to feel and judge the distance between his nose and the ground!

Chin: You can snip off the long hairs that grow under the chin and jaw-line.

Ears: You can carefully trim hair from the outside edges of the ears, but the inside is definitely a no-go area – that fuzz protects the delicate insides of the ear.

Poll: People like to cut a 'bridle-path' out of the mane behind the ears so the bridle head-piece can sit more neatly there.

Heels: It is not a good idea to trim the heels of an outdoor pony much in winter, as the long hair here generally helps to drain rain-water away. An exception is in areas of clay soil which clogs and sticks around the fetlocks. Use a mane comb to lift the hair the wrong way and cut it upwards.

Plaiting the tail

YOU will impress your friends if you can master this skill, which smartens up a pony with a full tail. Take a few hairs from each side at the top of the tail and fasten with thread. Using this as your centre strand, and a few more hairs from each side as your side strands, start to plait. Continue down the tail, taking more hairs from the sides, and keeping the plait tight and flat in the middle of the tail. When you reach the end of the tail-bone, just keep plaiting to the end of the long hairs. Secure this with thread or a band, loop it up to the bottom of the plait and stitch it so it lies flat.

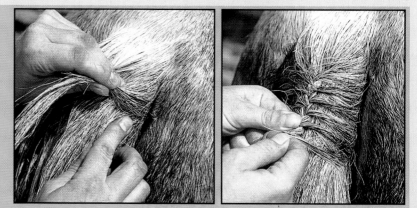

Pulling the mane and tail

MANES and tails can be tidied up by thinning them out. This is called 'pulling', and although it does involve pulling out hairs it isn't as painful as it sounds. It is best not to pull the tail of any pony that spends time out in the field, as the thickness helps to protect him against the cold wind and rain. All ponies can have their manes pulled, just remember not to take too much out if your pony lives outdoors as his thick mane helps keep his neck warm. Leave pulling until a mild day, after you have come back from a ride when the skin will be warm and the pores open. Using a proper pulling comb, take a few hairs from underneath the mane. Wrap them around the comb and pull sharply. Only do a few at a time or you will make your pony sore.

& Plaiting

THERE'S nothing like a neat row of plaits to really show off on those special occasions. Plaiting is quite an art, but practice makes perfect, so have a go and you will soon be producing some really top knots!

How to plait a mane

1 Tie your pony up. It really helps to make tidy plaits if your pony's mane is not too thick and long, so shorten and thin it by careful pulling (see left). Now brush the mane out thoroughly to one side and damp it down with a water brush. Divide it into equal sections, one for each plait. Make the partings as neat as you can with no stray hairs. Fasten each bunch loosely with an elastic band.

2 Here goes... Stand well above your pony on something safe, and take the first bunch. Divide it into three equal strands. Holding the hair slightly up and away from the crest, plait to the bottom by taking the right-hand strand over the centre one, then the left over the centre and so on. Pull the plait tight as you go.

3 At the end, hold the plait firmly. Take your rubber band and wind it around several times. Hold on tight or it will unravel! Tuck away any loose hairs neatly under the band.

4 Now fold the plait in half keeping the end underneath, then in half again to create a 'bobble'. Take another band and twist it tightly round the whole bobble several times to secure it to the crest.

5 Do each bunch one by one in this way until the whole mane is plaited, then finish with the forelock to complete the picture.

TIP

THERE are no hard and fast rules about how many plaits you do, but tradition says there should be an odd number down the neck plus one for the forelock.

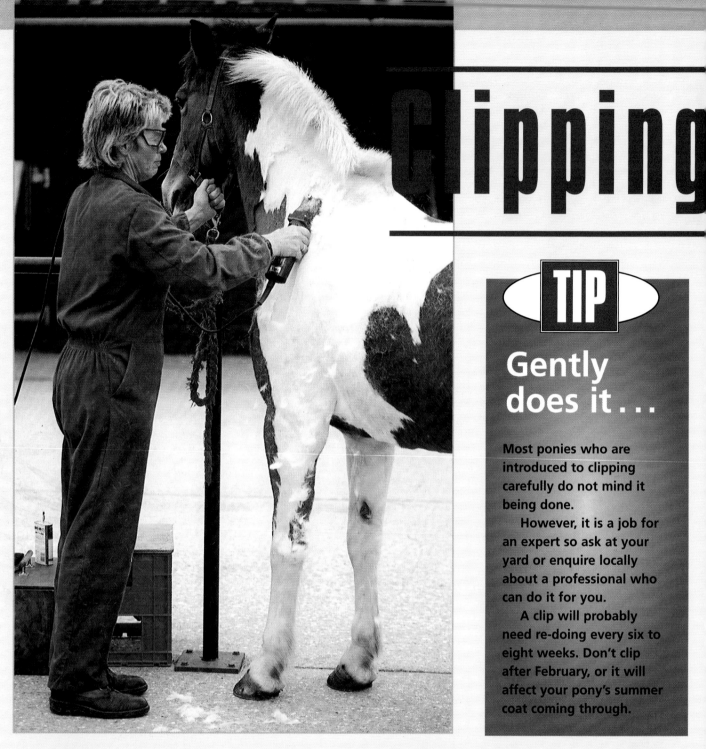

Clipping

TIP

Gently does it...

Most ponies who are introduced to clipping carefully do not mind it being done.

However, it is a job for an expert so ask at your yard or enquire locally about a professional who can do it for you.

A clip will probably need re-doing every six to eight weeks. Don't clip after February, or it will affect your pony's summer coat coming through.

Why your pony might need a clip

BY THE time autumn comes around, most ponies have begun to grow the thick, woolly coats designed to protect them against the cold, wet weather that is on its way. Without that fuzz they would lose body warmth and weight very quickly. The trouble is, that while these winter woolies are great protection when a pony is out in the field, when out on a ride – especially on milder days – it is like hiking in a fur-coat.

Sweating a lot is not good for a pony and will soon make him lose condition. Drying off a sweaty pony is a real chore, and dried-on sweat causes rubs and is

hard to brush off. By clipping away part of the winter coat the pony can be kept comfortable while he is working, and grooming will be easier.

But whoa – not every pony would benefit from clipping. Whether you need to clip, and the style you choose, depends on how your pony lives and the work he does. There is no point clipping off your pony's natural warmth-layer only to pile on more rugs and give more feed unnecessarily. Remember, a pony without his coat could get very cold indeed, especially if he lives out. Any hair taken off must be replaced by rugs (see page 36).

Hints

Types of clip

Neck and belly clip

For ponies ridden at weekends and holidays only. Can be used on a pony living out, with a New Zealand rug. If your pony is only ridden occasionally in winter, he is better off not clipped.

Trace clip

Can be low, medium or high, depending on how much is taken off. Suitable for ponies in regular work. Leaving the neck partially untrimmed is best for ponies that feel the cold.

Chaser clip

Suits ponies as for trace clip.

Blanket clip

Hair is left on the back and quarters like a blanket. Best for hard-working ponies who are kept mainly stabled.

Hunter clip

Only the saddle patch and legs are left untrimmed. Suitable only for very hard-working ponies who don't spend much time in the field. A pony with this clip must be well rugged up if he is turned out.

DEPENDING on your pony's lifestyle, you may need to buy rugs to help keep him warm in winter. Tough and hardy native ponies grow incredibly thick coats that give them better weather protection than any rug. If your pony is of this type, he is not clipped, and has good shelter in his field, there may be no need for him to wear a rug. However, other types of pony who live out will appreciate wearing an outdoor rug and will certainly need one if they are clipped.

Rugs:

New Zealand Rug

THIS is the rug that is worn outdoors. It is made of waterproof fabric, which was traditionally thick canvas, though now most modern rugs are made of lighter-weight man-made materials.

New Zealands have to fit well to make sure they stay in place whatever your pony fancies doing out in the field, including rolling, bucking and having a gallop! Old-fashioned rugs used to have a surcingle round the girth, but this uncomfortable style has now been replaced by either cross-surcingles under the belly or leg straps that cross between the hindlegs, or a combination of both.

A New Zealand should be deep enough to keep out the wind, and it should be big enough to give your pony freedom of movement and not cause rubs. But it should not be so loose and baggy that it lets in draughts or slips around. Remember, canvas rugs will need re-waterproofing after every winter.

The rug must be well-fitted, not to inhibit movement (left) ... in case your pony decides to gallop or roll (above).

Types

THE other main sort of rug you may need is a stable rug, which is worn when your pony comes indoors. Even if your pony is unclipped, if he is stabled he cannot move around much, so he may get cold in chilly weather without a rug on.

Most modern stable rugs are made of synthetic materials, often quilted, and fasten using surcingles that cross under the belly. In the past, rugs used to be secured using a wide strap called a roller around the girth. But this could easily put pressure on the spine and was not very comfortable for the horse or pony.

In very cold weather, or following a clip, you

Stable Rug

may need to add extra layers underneath a stable rug. You can either use an under-rug with its own fastenings, or a blanket. If you use a blanket it will need to be kept in place using a roller over the top of all the layers. Fasten the roller firmly but not over-tight, using a thick pad over the pony's backbone if the roller is not the kind that is styled to stay clear of the spine.

Other types

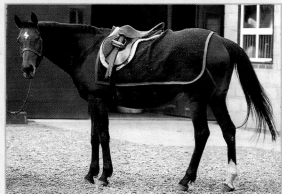

SUMMER SHEET

THIS is usually made of a cotton mix and is a lightweight sheet used in summer for travelling, or for keeping the dust and flies off.

Some types are 'coolers', designed to help a sweaty pony dry quickly. These can also be used under a stable rug to keep its lining clean.

SWEAT RUG

THE string-vest kind of rug you will often see on ponies at shows or slung over racehorses in the winner's enclosure. It works by trapping pockets of air, which then allow the horse to cool without getting cold. It can only do this if the air is trapped, so it must always be used with another rug on top. In warm weather this could be a cotton summer sheet, or in colder weather, a woollen travel rug or stable rug would be suitable.

TRAVEL RUG

A smart rug, usually made of wool, used for travelling in winter.

EXERCISE SHEET

A USEFUL addition to any pony's wardrobe. If you fasten on an exercise sheet (which may be either wool or lined with a waterproof fabric) under the saddle, it can keep off the rain during a winter ride. That means you will arrive home dry and you can pop your pony's New Zealand or stable rug straight back on.

Rugs:

RUGS range in size from about 4ft 6ins (138cms) for a tiny pony to 6ft (182cms) for a small horse. To get approximately the right size for your pony, measure from the point of the chest (between the forelegs) all the way along the body to the point of the buttock (below the tail). The rug should be long enough to just cover the tail and the buttocks, and deep enough to go well below the belly and elbows. A well-fitted rug sits neatly over the shoulders and follows the line of the back.

JUST like everything where ponies are concerned, there is a right way and wrong way of putting on and taking off rugs – both for safety's sake and for the pony's comfort!

1 Fold the rug in half so you can hold it up clear of the floor and keep it under control. You do not want it flapping around alarming your pony.

2 Put it over the pony well forwards, still folded. Fasten the front straps (inset).

3 Fold it back, adjust it and fasten the belly straps or hind-leg straps. Pull back slightly into place.

4 On a New Zealand rug, cross the hind leg straps over to keep the rug in place and stop it rubbing the legs (pictured, right).

Fitting

How to put on a rug

To put on a blanket underneath a stable rug (above), place it over the pony. Now fold the front corners up to the withers. Put the outer rug on top and fasten. Now fold back the 'V' of the blanket and fasten it underneath the roller. Make sure the roller has no twists in and is well clear of the spine.

Taking it off ...

WHEN taking off a rug you work in the opposite direction, back towards front. Undo the straps nearest the pony's back end first, then the belly and front ones. Either fold the rug forwards and slip it off from the side, or stand by the quarters and slip it off backwards with the lie of the hair.

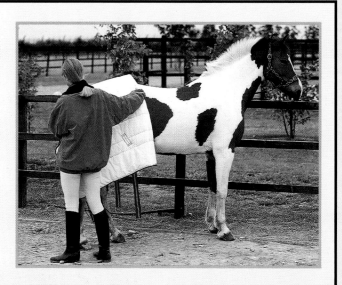

Shoeing

THROUGHOUT evolution the horse has relied upon his feet to carry him swiftly out of danger. Like our fingernails, the hooves grow continually, but by being forever on the move, over rough ground, the wild horse's tough feet wore naturally into shape.

It is equally important to the domesticated horse or pony to have healthy feet. But living in a stable or small field, their hooves would soon grow long and cracked, making the pony uncomfortable and unbalanced if they were not regularly trimmed back. However, riding – especially on a very hard surface like a road – wears down the feet faster than they can grow, which is why most riding horses and ponies need to wear metal shoes to stop their feet getting sore.

Trimming the feet and shoeing are the jobs of the farrier, an extremely skilled craftsman who trains for many years before being qualified to shoe. Although a pony's foot might look hard and dead from the outside, beneath the outer horn or hoof wall lie layers of super-sensitive tissues and nerves, and the crucial bones which keep the horse on its feet.

'No foot, no horse' is a true saying. Imagine if you tried to run and jump in tight or uncomfortable shoes...

When to call the farrier

MOST ponies will need the farrier every six to eight weeks. Even if the shoes are not loose or worn, don't leave it much longer than this as the feet will have grown too long for the shoes. If necessary, the farrier can trim the hooves back and replace the old shoes, saving you some cost – this is called removes. Here are some signs that a pony needs the farrier:

● The shoes are thin and worn.
● The toes or heels are over-growing the shoe, or the foot is starting to look long and flat.
● A shoe is loose or twisted, or has been lost.
● Your pony has started stumbling more than usual.

A well-shod foot

HERE are some things to look out for in a well-shod foot:

■ The shoe has been made to fit the foot – never the other way around!
■ There is no daylight between the foot and shoe.
■ The clenches are evenly spaced and level.
■ The frog is still in contact with the ground – this is the pony's anti-slip device.
■ The heels of the shoe are not too long.
■ The foot has been evenly trimmed at both the toe and heel.

Hot shoe for a better fit

IT IS very important that your pony's shoes fit him, as he will not be able to move comfortably if they do not. Most farriers shoe 'hot', as below, because this tends to give the best fit. It is possible to shoe 'cold', without heating the shoe, but fewer adjustments can be made to a cold shoe. Although a good fit is still possible, as a rule 'hot' shoeing is better.

From left: Taking off the old shoe using a buffer and hammer; the drawing knife is used to trim away overgrown hoof wall; the new shoe is heated in the forge and hammered into shape; the nails are hammered through the dead 'wall' of the foot.

Step-by-step...

1 Firstly your farrier will look at each foot to see how the old shoes have been worn. He then uses his buffer and hammer to cut off the heads of the old nails (called clenches), and levers the shoe off with his pincers.

2 Next he trims off over-grown horn with his hoof clippers and drawing knife, and smooths off the edges with a huge nail file called a rasp.

3 He takes a shoe that is about the right size and holds it against the foot. It will probably need altering to fit, so this is done by placing it in the forge until the metal is red-hot and soft, then banging it into shape on the anvil. The hot shoe is carried using the pritchel.

4 While it is still hot, the shoe is tried on the foot again. This looks (and smells!) alarming and makes lots of smoke, but it does not hurt the pony. The hot shoe leaves a burn mark on the horn which shows if it is sitting evenly and is the correct shape. Clips are made to help keep the shoe in place on the foot – usually one on the front of a fore-shoe and two 'quarter clips' on a hind-shoe.

5 More adjustments are made if necessary. When it is ready, the shoe is cooled and fastened on the foot by driving nails through the hoof wall, where the pony has no feeling. The tips of the nails which stick out (clenches) are turned over, clipped off and hammered down. Usually four nails are used on the outside of the foot and three on the inside – the area towards the heel is left to allow it to expand slightly as the pony moves.

6 Finally, the rasp smooths off the join between the foot and shoe (picture, left).

Fit &

G IVEN all the right care and attention, your pony will be happy and healthy. But even the best looked-after pony might become ill or injure himself at some point. With some knowledgeable help, you may be able to deal with minor problems yourself, but if you are in any doubt – and always, in certain circumstances – get the vet straight away or something small could become a big problem in no time at all. Knowing how your pony looks and behaves when he's feeling well, and recognising the signs of a sick or unhealthy pony, means you can pick up on trouble quickly and know when to call the vet.

A well cared-for, healthy pony has:

● A shine to his coat. It should not be dull and starey (though, remember his thick winter fur is never going to really gleam!)

● Bright eyes.

● An interest in his surroundings, with ears flicking to and fro.

● A good appetite and drinks regularly.

● Loose, supple skin, which is not tight.

● A body filled with good muscle tone – not fat, or thin with bones protruding.

● Moist, pink membranes to his eyes, nose and mouth – these should not be pale or dry.

● Regular droppings, not very hard or loose.

● Clear urine, passed regularly without strain.

● No puffiness or heat in the legs, weight evenly distributed on all four feet.

● No cough, discharge from the nostrils, or swollen glands.

● Normal breathing and temperature.

Pulse rate

This should be 36-42 beats per minute. Place two fingers (not your thumb) on the artery running inside the jaw, inside the foreleg or behind the eye.

Temperature

Normal temperature is 38 deg C (100.5 F). It is taken by inserting a greased thermometer into the rectum for one minute. Call the vet if it is one degree or more above or below.

Breathing rate

This should be 8-12 breaths per minute. Watch the flanks of a pony at rest.

Make a note of your pony's normal pulse and breathing rates so you can compare them if you are worried. Wait a while after exercise for readings to be accurate.

Healthy

Routine Health Care

Prevention is always better than cure. There are three aspects of routine care that will go a long way towards keeping your pony healthy and stop problems in their tracks before they occur. These are worming and vaccination programmes, and routine teeth rasping.

WORMING

ALL horses and ponies carry internal parasites in their gut called worms. You will never be able to get rid of them completely because the pony eats the worm eggs with his grass all the time. But you can keep them under control with medication and good pasture management. If a pony is not wormed regularly, larvae grow inside his stomach and intestines. He'll lose weight and risk serious stomach ache. A pony with worms will have a dull coat and be thin, with a pot-belly.

◆ Worm regularly every six to eight weeks. You can get wormers from your vet or tack shop.
◆ Use either a paste in a syringe, or powder given in the feed (as above). Follow the manufacturer's instructions about dose carefully.
◆ Worm all ponies that share a field together at the same time.
◆ Make sure the brand you use deals with all types of parasites.
◆ Keep worms at bay by picking up droppings from the field every week.

JABS

PONIES are at risk from two serious highly infectious diseases – tetanus and equine flu – that can be prevented by one simple vaccination by your vet. Your pony will need a course of two jabs, followed by yearly boosters. Both vaccinations can be given in one injection.

TEETH RASPING

UNLIKE our own gnashers, ponies' teeth grow all the time and get continuously worn down as they chew on their diet of grass. Trouble brews because the grinding teeth at the back (the molars) often wear unevenly, creating sharp edges that then cut the sides of the mouth, especially when there is a bit in there. This can be very painful and, not surprisingly, causes no

end of riding problems. It can also stop the pony digesting his food properly. Make sure your pony's teeth never cause bother by asking the vet to rasp them (file the edges off) every six months.

Common

WELL-CARED-FOR ponies, on the whole, keep very healthy so there is no need to be alarmed by this list of 'common' ailments. But knowing something about the various problems that can crop up will help you avoid them, and to take the right steps if they do occur.

ANY pain or discomfort in a pony's foot, leg or joints could make him limp or 'go lame'. Lameness can be caused by injury or by disease.

Sometimes it is very obvious, but on other occasions it might be very slight and barely noticeable. If your pony is lame, or you suspect he is, run your hand carefully down each leg feeling for any wound, heat or swelling.

Pick up each foot in turn, see if it feels hot, and look carefully for anything that might be stuck in the sole.

If you cannot find any obvious cause, or you are unsure which leg has the problem, you will need to 'trot him up' and ask someone knowledgeable to watch your pony move.

Trotting up

A pony should walk taking rhythmical steps of the same length. If he does not, there is lameness in one or more legs.

Tell-tale signs of lameness

Lameness often does not show much in walk, so trot the pony away from the person watching, in a straight line. Turn the pony away from you (on your inside), then trot back and past your observer.

Do not hold the pony's head too closely, as the head position will help show you which leg is sore.

If the pony is lame on a foreleg, he will dip his head as his sound foot goes down on the ground. If he is lame on a hindleg, his quarters will dip more as his sound foot goes down.

You may have spotted a wound, bump or something in the foot. If so, it is time to use your first aid skills (see page 48). But if the lameness is very severe, or you have doubts about what is causing it, bring your pony in and call the vet.

Thrush

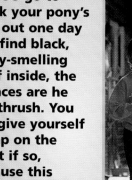

IF YOU go to pick your pony's feet out one day and find black, nasty-smelling stuff inside, the chances are he has thrush. You can give yourself a slap on the wrist if so, because this infection usually is caused by the pony standing around in wet and dirty bedding. Wash his feet out thoroughly with an antiseptic scrub, then spray the sole with an antibiotic spray – and keep his feet very clean!

Ailments

Colic

THIS is any kind of horsey 'tummy-ache', and it is very painful. For some reason, the pony is unable to digest its food properly because, somewhere along the line, there is a problem. And, as we know the pony's insides are long and delicate, colic is always serious. Ring the vet straight away and ask his advice on how to deal with your pony until he arrives.

Any kind of feeding mistake can set off colic, though one of the commonest causes is worm damage. Early warning signs include dullness, sweating and a raised temperature, and restlessness, with the pony biting at or trying to kick his flanks and being off his food. Do not let a pony with colic roll, even if he wants to, as he may suffer a fatal twisted gut.

Strangles

STRANGLES is a very infectious disease. It is uncommon, but it can be caught by young ponies, often from a new horse coming into a yard. The pony will look very ill and have very swollen throat glands. Isolate him in a comfortable stable, keep him warm and call the vet.

Laminitis

PONIES are especially prone to this painful, crippling disease which can make them very lame indeed, usually in both fore-feet or both hind-feet at the same time, making them stand leaning back like a rocking-horse.

One of the main causes is a pony being allowed to over-indulge himself on the feeding front – and that might mean eating too much grass, particularly the lush spring variety, or too much hard feed.

There are other causes that contribute to laminitis, such as jarring from hard ground or a blood imbalance, but over-feeding is the usual culprit – and so preventing this awful condition is down to you! Be cruel to be kind to ponies, particularly in the spring and summer, restricting their grazing if needs be.

What happens in laminitis is the joined layers of sensitive and insensitive laminae inside the foot split apart, making the main bone of the foot – the pedal bone – turn and drop downwards, sometimes even through the sole. Laminitis is always very serious. If you suspect your pony is having an attack – usually signalled by a high temperature and difficulty in moving – stable him and call the vet immediately for treatment and advice on his diet and care.

Common

If your pony has a tendency to cough, use dust-free bedding, such as shavings.

How to beat the cough

GO TO any large yard in winter and you are sure to hear one or more of the occupants coughing. All ponies will occasionally clear their throats with a cough, particularly when starting off a ride. But a persistent cough, or one accompanied by a runny nose, means trouble and can soon run a pony down.

Coughing can have many causes but the two most common are infection and allergy. Infection may be a cold or equine flu, both of which cause a high temperature and dullness and need the vet.

Mud fever

A SOGGY winter and a boggy field will put ponies at risk from cracked heels and mud fever. These are fungal infections that get into the skin when it becomes waterlogged and chapped or scratched. The telltale signs are that the skin becomes red and sore and then splits, or goes scabby, causing painful sores.

Act on the first signs of mud fever or cracked heels before they get worse. You will need to trim back the hair and (carefully!) pick off any scabs to let the air get to the skin. Now wash the legs gently with a medicated cleanser. Let them dry completely before rubbing in some zinc-based cream – nappy rash creams are brilliant for this! Keep the legs as dry as possible until the area is healed. If you can, bring the pony in, but if this is not possible, use a barrier cream like udder cream on the dry legs before turning out again.

Continually washing mud off legs in cold weather seems to make a pony more likely to get mud fever. Always wait for the mud to dry, then gently brush it off. If you must wash the legs, dry them thoroughly before turning your pony out again.

Rain scald is a mud fever-type infection that affects the back during wet weather. Treat in the same way – then give your pony better protection against the rain!

Ailments

But most cases of coughing are down to the pony being sensitive to the dust and spores in all hay and straw. This is called COPD – chronic obstructive pulmonary disease – and is very common.

The vet can give medication to help with serious cases, but generally this is a problem you can deal with yourself by some changes to your pony's management.

Basically, the pony needs as much fresh air as you can give him. If you can, turn him out all the time. If this is not possible, then let him spend as much time as you can in the field, and when he has to come in, make sure he has a very airy, well-ventilated stable. Use dust-free bedding such as shavings or paper. Replace hay by haylage, or soak the hay-net for a few hours, allowing the dust and spores to swell, so they do not go down into his lungs.

Damp all hard feeds too. And remember, it's no use taking all these measures if the stable next door has heaps of straw and hay in it!

Sweet itch

SWEET itch can make summer miserable for some ponies who spend their whole time itching and scratching away at the irritation on their manes and tails, often rubbing them bare. As it is thought to be caused by an allergy to the biting of certain mosquitoes, the best way to avoid and treat it is to make sure pony and 'mozzies' meet up as little as possible!

Keep your pony inside at the worst time for midges, in the morning and evening. At all times, put on lots of fly repellent and renew it frequently. Avoid putting a sweet-itch prone pony out into a field with a stream, river, pond or ditch in it.

You can get benzyl benzoate lotion from your vet to help soothe your pony's itchy areas, or in bad cases he may be able to prescribe something stronger.

ANY sick pony feels much like you do when you are ill – absolutely lousy. So if your pony is ill, treat him as you would want to be treated. Make him comfortable, keep him warm and don't fuss around him too much. Follow all your vet's instructions. Cut any hard feed right down and just give him hay, replacing his usual concentrates with a few handfuls of tasty chaff, apples and carrots or a special 'invalid' mix.

PERHAPS because they are big animals that move about a lot, often quite fast, and take fright easily, ponies are always getting into scrapes! There are going to be times when your pony gets a cut or a knock. You can deal with minor injuries like this yourself with some basic first aid, but however small a cut or graze may seem, never ignore it as it can easily become infected.

Make a point of checking your pony over closely every day for cuts, particularly on his legs, and clean up and treat any injury you find without delay.

Step by Step

How to treat a wound

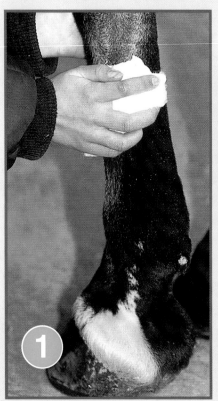

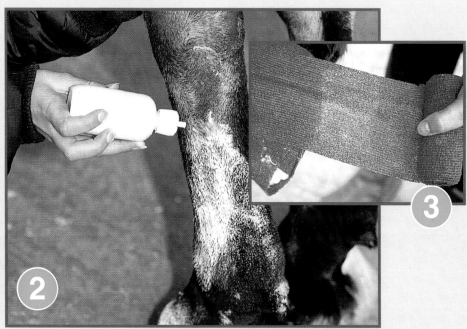

1 Take a pad of cotton-wool and some clean, slightly salted water. Clean the wound carefully, letting the water drip on to it first, then wiping away from it and using a fresh piece of cotton wool with each wipe. Bruising and swelling can be reduced by some (careful!) gentle hosing.

2 Puff with wound powder or spray with antibiotic wound spray. Tiny cuts can be left uncovered, but should be cleaned regularly until they heal.

3 Larger wounds or scrapes will need bandaging as long as they are in a place where you can bandage – i.e. the lower leg. Don't try to bandage other parts of the body – keep the wounds clean.

4 If the wound is deep, or more than 2cm long, clean it as best you can and then leave it alone and call the vet – it may need stitching and antibiotics.

5 To stop bleeding, apply pressure to the wound with a clean gauze pad. If bleeding continues, pad and bandage then call the vet right away.

Aid

Types of wound

- Tear, e.g. on some barbed wire.
- Lacerated, straightforward cut, e.g. on plain wire.
- Puncture, when the skin is pierced, e.g. when horse treads on a nail.
- Sores, caused by rubbing or chafing.
- Bruising, where the skin is not broken but there is bleeding and swelling underneath.

Get yourself kitted out

KEEP a well-stocked first aid kit at the yard and remember to take it to shows, too. You never know when you might need it. It should contain:

- Thermometer
- Plenty of crepe bandages
- Scissors
- Safety pins or sticky plaster tape
- Gauze pads
- Poultice
- Roll of cotton wool
- Wound powder
- Roll of Gamgee
- Antibiotic spray
- Dressings
- Bowl

A PUNCTURE wound is especially dangerous because it is hard to see, but dirt and germs may have been forced deep into the skin and trapped there. The infection has to be drawn out of the wound using a poultice. The most likely time you may need a poultice is if your pony steps on to something sharp like a thorn, nail or a piece of glass, which pierces his sole. He will be very lame, and if there is infection inside, his foot will be hot and sore. If this happens:

1 Call your vet or farrier to come and find the spot and pare away some sole to release any infection building up inside.

2 Boil some water and allow it to cool to body temperature (feel it to make sure!).

3 Cut your poultice to the right size – big enough to cover the whole area.

4 Put it on the foot (or other wound) with the sticky side down.

5 Cover the whole foot with a plastic bag, cling film, or an 'equiboot'.

6 Bandage this on securely, then put it in another bag and secure with a bandage.

REMEMBER – Poultices must be changed twice a day and used for at least two days after your pony is sound and there is no more discharge.

IF you find a sore or saddle 'gall' on your pony where his tack has been rubbing, give yourself a black mark, because properly-fitted tack on a clean pony should never cause him discomfort like this.

- Check your tack and get advice about how it is fitted. Do not use it again until you are sure it fits correctly. Keep tack clean and supple, and always brush your pony in the areas where his tack goes before riding.

- Do not ride until the sores have healed. Clean the area (as for Wounds) and spray on antiseptic.

THE BRIDLE is a set of straps that fasten round the pony's head and support the bit in his mouth. The reins, attached to the rings of the bit, are your communication lines with your pony. The bit sits over the tongue in the gap between the pony's front and back teeth. Most bits are made of stainless steel, though the mouthpiece is sometimes rubber or plastic. There are many kinds of bit and each type works in a slightly different way. Most ponies wear a simple snaffle bit, with or without a joint in the centre. It might have 'loose' rings that slide through the mouthpiece, or fixed 'eggbutt' rings. Stronger ponies may need a 'curb' bit with a curb chain, such as a Pelham. Do not change your bit without asking the advice of your instructor.

TACK, or saddlery, is the name given to all the gear a pony wears when it is ridden. Every rider needs to learn about the different items of tack, how they fit and why a pony has them. Each has a special use, but the two main pieces of equipment every pony wears are a saddle and a bridle. To be safe, effective and comfortable for you and your pony, all tack must fit well and be put on properly every time you ride.

Tack:

You cannot use any old bit on your pony. His bit must fit him well if it is to work properly and not hurt his mouth. When the bridle is on and the bit is at the right height, there should be just half a centimetre of mouthpiece showing between his lips and the bit-ring (just enough to fit your finger in).

Step by Step

How to put on a bridle ...

1 If you are not in the stable, fasten the head collar around the pony's neck.

2 Facing forwards, stand close to the pony's near (left) side and put the reins over his head. Hold the bridle so the bit is in front of his mouth, then guide it in with your left hand. If he is awkward, you may have to slip your thumb into the side of the gums, where there aren't any teeth, to encourage him to open up.

3 Carefully bring the headpiece up over the ears, one by one. Then pull out the forelock and tidy the mane. Check the bit is at a comfortable height – it should just wrinkle the lips as if the pony is smiling. It must not be too low and droopy so it knocks on the teeth, or too high and tight – ouch! You can adjust it using the cheekpieces.

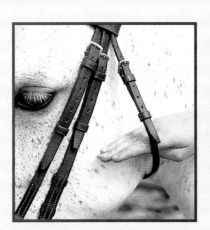

4 Buckle the throatlash, making sure that four fingers will easily fit between the pony's cheek and the strap. Check the noseband is lying underneath the cheekpeices and is sitting level, midway between the pony's cheekbones and the bit. Fasten the noseband snugly but leave space for two fingers to slip underneath. Make sure all the straps are securely in their keepers.

The Bridle & Bit

Parts of the bridle

... and how to take it off again properly

1 Undo the throatlash and noseband.
2 Ease the headpiece over the ears. Gently slip the bit out, taking care not to bang the teeth
3 Put on the pony's headcollar, then bring the reins over the head.

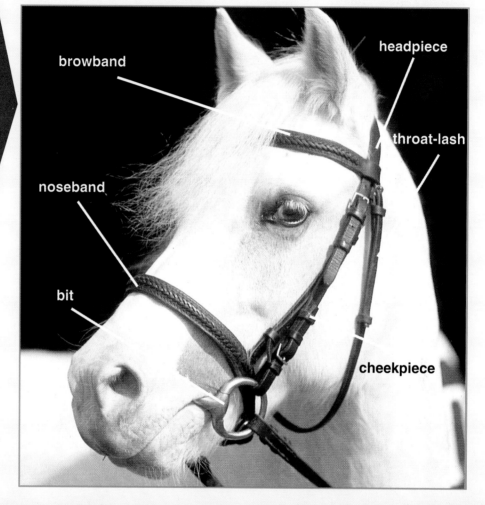

browband

headpiece

throat-lash

noseband

bit

cheekpiece

The Noseband

MOST bridles have an ordinary cavesson noseband that sits above the bit (above). It is possible to gain extra control over a pony that tries to open his mouth to avoid the action of the bit by using a 'drop' type of noseband that fits below the bit.

This could either be a traditional drop noseband, a Flash noseband, made up of a cavesson plus a drop strap, or a crossed or Grakle noseband.

If you use a dropped noseband of any kind, make sure it is fitted well up, so it does not squeeze on the soft part of the pony's nose and hamper his breathing. Fasten it snugly, but not crunchingly tight, making sure the lips are not pinched.

THE saddle is what keeps you sitting securely on your pony's back in the right position, so you can give the aids with your legs in the correct place on his sides and stay in balance as he moves. There are several different kinds of specialist saddles designed for particular activities, but for everyday riding you will use a 'general purpose' one.

Saddles were traditionally always made of leather, but it is now possible to choose between leather and synthetic saddles, which are handy for pony owners because they are very lightweight, tough, easy to clean and cost less. All saddles are built around a wooden or plastic frame called a 'tree'. The tree's cushioned panels help to place your weight evenly, making it easier for your pony to carry you.

The stirrups are not attached to the saddle but hang by straps, called the leathers, from the bars of the tree, under the skirt. The girth, which can be made of leather, cotton or webbing, fits around the pony's belly to hold everything in place. A numnah is a saddle-shaped pad that fits underneath for extra comfort and to help absorb sweat.

Tack:

Saddle fit

GETTING a good fit of saddle for your pony is crucial – a badly-fitting saddle can do a lot of damage to a pony's back. It is worth taking time to make sure it fits well. Don't presume that any saddle will fit any pony, as ponies come in all shapes and sizes. If your new pony comes with a saddle, it may not necessarily fit, because, even if it once did, ponies can change shape.

Ask a professional saddler to come and check it out for you. You may not need to buy a new one – it might just need re-stuffing inside by the saddler. When buying a new saddle, always have it fitted to the pony first.

Here are some checks to see if your saddle is OK for your pony, or if it may need re-stuffing or replacing. All saddles do need re-stuffing from time to time.

● When it is in the right place on the pony's back, the saddle should sit evenly – not really high at the front or at the back. It should not move around a lot as the pony moves (though there will be some movement).

● With a rider on board, there should still be plenty of daylight visible all the way along the gullet, front to back. You should be able to fit four fingers easily into the gullet at the front

and at least three fingers' width at the back. The gullet should be wide enough to sit either side of the withers, and you need to be able to get your fingers under the padding here quite easily – if it is tight, it will be pinching.

● Check for a broken tree, too. Hold the saddle with the pommel in your lap and use both hands to pull the cantle towards you. There should only be the tiniest amount of 'give' due to springiness built into the tree. If it creaks or really moves, the tree is broken – bin it!

● Lumpy or very soft panels mean it's time for re-stuffing.

1 IF you are not in a stable, tie your pony up, or have someone hold him. Hold the saddle with your left hand on the pommel and your right hand under the seat. Standing on the near (left) side place the saddle gently on the highest part of the withers.

Step by Step

2 NOW slide it down to the correct position and pull the numnah up into the gullet.

How to put on a saddle

2

Saddles

3 GO round the front of the pony to the other side and let the girth down. Back on the near side, take the girth from under the belly, ensuring there are no twists, then buckle it up to the girth straps beneath the saddle flaps – gently! You will have to tighten it up later, as most ponies puff themselves out at first. Use either the first two straps or outside two.

3

4 PULL down the buckle guard. Take each fore-leg in turn and pull it forwards, to ease out any wrinkles under the girth. Only run the stirrups down the leathers when you are ready to ride.

4

Taking it off ...

1 Make sure the stirrup irons are run up. Undo the girth on the near side.

2 Go around to the off-side and put the girth up over the saddle.

3 Back on the near side, lift the saddle well clear of the pony's back. Put it down carefully somewhere safe. Rub the pony's back to help get the circulation going again.

Martingales

Carry it properly

ANOTHER piece of tack your pony might wear is a martingale. This is a combination of neck strap with other straps running from it to the bridle or reins, and to the girth. Martingales are used to stop the pony throwing his head up so high that it makes riding difficult.

A running martingale divides into two straps with a ring on each end, through which each rein is threaded. To keep it in position it should always be used with rubber stops in front of the rings on the reins, and one where the straps join at the chest. It must be fitted right, or it will either be no use at all, or will restrict the pony too much. Free the reins and hold the martingale straps up towards the pony's withers – they should reach to about a hand's width away.

A standing martingale (above) has one broad strap that fastens directly to a cavesson noseband (never to a drop-type noseband). For the right fit, push the strap up into the pony's gullet. It should comfortably go right up to the throatlash.

YOUR tack, and especially your saddle, is the most expensive equipment you own – besides the pony himself. If you take good care of your saddlery it will last years, but it is very easily damaged – and damaged tack can be unsafe and bad news for you and your pony.

NOT many pony owners like cleaning tack, but it's a chore you need to make yourself do at least once a week. If you are very keen, a clean after every ride would earn top marks! It is important to clean tack regularly, because grease soon builds up on it, which can cause rubs and sores on your pony's skin, and it make the stitching rot so it becomes unsafe. Leather that is hardly ever soaped gets stiff and cracked, and is liable to break at any time.

Keeping your tack CLEAN

Step by Step

THIS quick clean need only take a few minutes. Try to do a more complete job every week or so, when you will need to take all the pieces apart and clean them thoroughly.

1 Hang up the bridle to clean it, and put the saddle on a saddle horse (right) or over your knee.

2 Equip yourself with a small bucket of clean, warm water, some saddle soap, a cloth and a few sponges. An old toothbrush is handy for scrubbing the bit, stirrup irons and treads.

3 Use the cloth to wipe the bit and stirrup irons. Rinse it out and wipe all the leatherwork over on both sides, making sure you shift all the grease you can see. Tough spots (called 'jockeys') may need a bit of help from your fingernail. Don't get the leather too wet.

4 Now take the saddle soap and dip it in the water. Rub the sponge into it, trying not to make too much lather. Soap the leather all over with the sponge. Finish with a final polish from a soft, dry cloth.

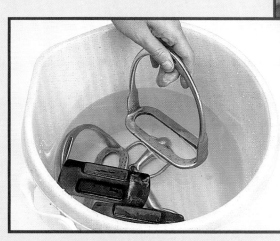

TIP

IF your leather tack gets wet, never put it by the fire or radiator. Let it dry out naturally or it will crack and break!

5 Don't forget your cotton girth and numnah – there's nothing nastier for your pony than having to keep wearing the same greasy, sweaty ones. It is easy to pop these in the washing-machine, and you can protect the machine from buckles by putting girths in an old pillow case. Nylon headcollars can be washed this way too, and lightweight stable rugs.

6 No excuses if you have got synthetic tack, which is very easy to clean. Simply wipe it over with a damp cloth, using dilute washing-up liquid to clear any greasy patches.

Riders need to recognise different boots and know how to use them.

Boots

Protection pointers

THERE are times when your pony's legs need some protection. Out riding, this could be because you are going to do some jumping where he may get a bump, or because his action tends to bring his legs a bit too close together and he sometimes knocks into himself. At these times boots are used to guard the legs. Riders need to know how to recognise the different sorts of boots and their uses. The most commonly-used boots for riding are:

Brushing boots

FOR: Exercise, jumping, especially cross-country.
FIT: Around the lower leg, fastened snugly but not too tight. You should be able to slip a finger down inside. Always fasten with the straps on the outside, pointing backwards. Front boots usually have four straps and hind boots have five straps.

Over-reach boots

FOR: Ponies that 'over-reach', i.e. over-step with their hind feet, catching the heels of the fore-feet.
FIT: On the fore-feet only. Some fit around the pastern and are tied with a strap (not too tight). Rubber boots need to be pulled on over the hoof. You might need a hoof pick or piece of string to get them on and off.

Tendon boots

FOR: Showjumping, or exercise if the pony is likely to strike into himself high up.
FIT: Used on forelegs only. The padded section of the boot sits around the tendons at the back of the lower leg. The straps go round the front, fastening on the outside, pointing

& Bandages

Bandaging is also used to protect a wound.

LEG protection can have other purposes too. Some competition riders use exercise bandages to guard and support their horse's tendons during work. Another kind of bandaging, using stable bandages, can be used to help keep a sick or tired horse's legs warm and supported in the stable, for protection during travelling, or to keep on a dressing over a wound or injury. Bandaging is, therefore, a useful skill for you to learn – though don't expect to do a perfect job first time!

Exercise bandages are narrow crepe bandages put on from under the knee or hock to just above the fetlock. Putting on exercise bandages properly is a very skilled job and badly-put on bandages could damage your pony's legs. If you want to give your pony extra leg protection for shows, competitions and out riding, it is better to be on the safe side and use brushing boots. When you are down by your pony's feet, always squat, never kneel or sit down – you may need to move in a hurry!

Stable bandages are wide bandages made from a soft, stretchy material like felt or wool. They are put on snugly but not tightly, over padding, from below the knee or hock right over the fetlock, around the pastern and up again.

CHECK LIST

1 Always use padding underneath any bandage. This can either be synthetic 'Fybagee' or a piece of Gamgee cut off a roll. Make sure it is the right size and is lying smoothly on the leg

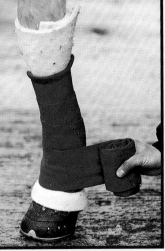

2 Have your bandage tightly rolled up ready. Start like this (above), then wind around, tucking in the flap with the next wind. Each turn should cover two thirds of the previous one.

3 When you reach the bottom, start bandaging upwards again. Aim to finish halfway up the leg if you can.

4 Fasten the bandage firmly. It might have Velcro or tapes that need tying. With tapes, do a double bow on the outside of the leg, never the front or back. Tuck in the ends. Make fastenings snug but not so tight they dig in.

5 Can you easily slip a finger down inside your bandage? If not, it is too tight, so try again.

6 Always bandage the legs in pairs – not just one fore leg or back leg. Even if only one is injured, the other leg will need a bandage for support.

Things you need to keep your pony safe

Travel boots

Special padded boots to guard against knocks or him treading on himself. Stable bandages can be used instead.

Tail bandage

Stops the pony leaning on the ramp and rubbing his tail raw. You can use just a tail bandage on its own.

Light rug

This is secured with a padded roller, which the tail guard fastens to. In hot weather a cool, thin rug protects against dust, flies and knocks. If your pony has been sweating or might get hot, put an anti-sweat sheet underneath then the other rug on top, folding back the front of the top rug and securing everything under the roller. This will keep him warm but stop him overheating.

Extras

This includes a poll guard (fits on the headcollar behind the ears in case of the pony throwing up his head and bumping it), over-reach boots, and knee and hock boots (fasten tightly above the knee/hock and loosely underneath, to protect these joints).

EVEN if you do not get to go to shows or Pony Club rallies very often, there are going to be times when your pony has to be transported somewhere in a trailer or horse-box. Travelling can be a risky and stressful time for a pony, but you can make it safer and easier for him by getting him well kitted out in protective gear, and knowing how to load, transport and unload him properly.

Hints

Six steps to putting on the perfect tail bandage

BESIDE travelling purposes, tail bandages can be used after grooming or any time you want to keep your pony's tail clean and neat. Remember not to leave a tail bandage on too long though – a few hours is quite long enough.

1 Brush the top of the tail with a damp water brush.

2 Take a narrow crepe exercise-type bandage. Stand slightly to one side of your pony's tail. Lift it gently and place a few inches of bandage underneath, keeping it flat.

3 Wind round once quite tightly. Tuck in the flap and wind round again, keeping the bandage flat and firm.

4 Now start winding down the tail keeping up an even pressure and covering a half to two-thirds of the previous turn each time.

5 Stop when you reach the end of the tail-bone. Now start going up the tail. Aim to finish half-way back up. Wind the tapes a few times around the tail firmly, then tie in a double bow. Tuck in the ends.

6 Bend the tail gently back into its natural shape.

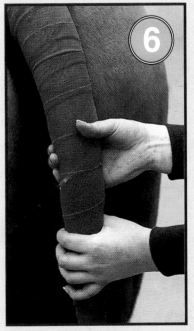

Taking it off...

TO take a tail bandage off, simply undo the tapes, take a hold of the top of the bandage and pull it firmly downwards.

ALWAYS give yourself plenty of time for loading, especially with a pony who is not very used to travelling. If you think about it, walking into an enclosed space is quite a frightening experience for a pony, so you need to be patient and give him confidence. If everyone keeps calm you should not have too many problems.

Loading tips

1 Recruit at least one, and preferably two helpers who are confident with horses.

2 Make the trailer/lorry as inviting as you can. Open any front doors to let the light in and have some straw or shavings on the floor. You can put some on the ramp too. Hang up a haynet securely.

3 Position the trailer or lorry alongside a wall. Have your pony kitted out ready to travel. Wear your riding hat and gloves, and some sensible boots or shoes.

4 Lead your pony straight to the centre of the ramp. Do not drag him along behind!

5 Walk just ahead of him into the trailer. Get a helper to immediately fasten the breech straps behind him and put up the ramp (carefully!). Now tie the lead-rope to the string on the tie ring. Give him enough rope to move his head up and down and reach the haynet easily, but not so much that he could try to turn around in a trailer with no partition.

6 Never travel two ponies in a trailer without a central partition. Never get inside the trailer when it is moving, and never go down alongside your pony in a partitioned trailer at any time – if he panics, you are trapped and there will be a nasty accident.

MOST ponies, who have never had a bad experience of travelling, will load well. However, some may be frightened or, occasionally, just plain naughty about loading. Keep calm and try these tips:

- Start off loading another pony first into the other side of a partitioned trailer. This might give him confidence that all is well in there.

- Put a bucket of food inside, just out of reach. But do not give him any until he has stepped on to the ramp, then make him step forwards for more. Try not to stand right in front of him with the bucket, as you will be blocking his way forwards.

- If your pony will stand at the base of the ramp calmly. Try picking up a foot and putting it down on the ramp.

- If all else fails, lunge lines usually do the trick. Take two lines and clip one end of each to string loops either side of the back of the trailer. Your two helpers need to walk past each other, crossing their lines behind the pony, keeping them well up over the hocks. Then they can slowly close the lines in, encouraging him forwards.

Hints

Towing tips for parents

■ Make sure your towing vehicle is up to the weight it has to pull.

■ The trailer must be regularly serviced.

■ When you hitch up, double-check the safety chain is over the tow-bar, the brake is off, the coupling is on correctly and all the electrics work.

■ Drive very slowly and carefully, especially around corners and roundabouts. Imagine there is a cup of tea on the dashboard! Allow plenty of room for turns.

■ Give yourself time and space to brake slowly.

■ If you are only carrying one pony in a partitioned trailer, load him into the inside side. He can balance better there, and will not be bumping along in the gutter.

Reluctant ones

Unloading

IF your trailer has a front-unload door, untie the pony, then undo the breast bar and lead him out slowly forwards, keeping his head down. If you are only going a short way you can travel your pony in his tack, but always put a rug on top, make sure the stirrups are up and the reins are threaded up out of the way through the bridle throatlash. Use a headcollar over the bridle for tying up and leading. The pony should be wearing travel boots.

With a rear-unload trailer, untie the pony and have a helper lower the ramp gently and undo the breech straps. Make your pony stand for a few seconds before asking him to step slowly backwards down the ramp, with you at his head, keeping him straight.

ANIMALINTEX: A type of poultice that can be used hot or cold and is very useful in a first aid kit.

BARS 1) The parts of the gums at the sides of the mouth where there are no teeth, where the bit lies. 2) Metal hooks that are part of the saddle tree, from which the stirrup leathers hang.

BOX-REST: When a sick pony has to stay in his stable until he has

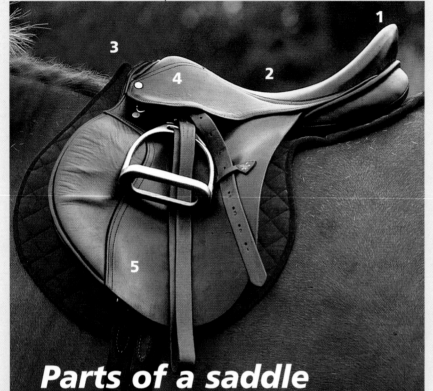

Parts of a saddle

1. Cantle
2. Seat
3. Pommel
4. Skirt
5. Saddle flap

recovered from illness or injury.

BREAKING OUT: When a pony starts sweating again after cooling off after exercise, because he has been kept too warm.

BRUSHING: A kind of 'interference', where the pony knocks into his leg with the opposite foot as he moves.

CAST: When a pony lies down and cannot get up.

CASTING A SHOE: Losing a shoe.

CAVESSON: 1) A simple type of noseband. 2) Special headgear with a ring fixed to the noseband for attaching a lungeing rein to.

CHAFF: Straw, or a mixture of hay and straw, chopped up and added to the feed to provide more fibre.

CLENCH: The part of the nail left sticking up out of the hoof wall after the shoe has been put on by

the farrier. He then bends it over and hammers the end down.

CLIP: 1) Shearing off part of the winter coat to stop a horse sweating during work. 2) The part of a horseshoe that turns over the edge of the foot to keep the shoe in place.

COLIC: Horsey stomach-ache.

CRIB-BITING A stable 'vice' caused by boredom, where the horse fixes his teeth onto any hard edge he can find.

CREST: The top edge of the neck, where plaits lie.

DISHING: A poor action, where the front feet are thrown out to the side.

DOCK: The top part of the tail, where the bone lies.

DROP NOSEBAND: A type of noseband that fits below the bit.

DUMPED TOE: Where a farrier has cut the toe too short to fit it to a shoe that is too small.

EGGBUTT: A T-shaped joint between the mouthpiece and rings of a bit, which stops the lips being pinched.

FARRIER: Someone trained to care for and fit shoes to a horse's feet.

FROG: The rubbery V-shaped structure in the centre of the sole under the foot.

FYBAGEE: A type of synthetic padding used under bandages.

GALL: A sore around the belly caused by a girth that is dirty or pinching the skin.

GAMGEE: A type of padding for under bandages made of cotton-wool lined by cotton mesh.

GRAZING: The pasture where a pony is turned out to graze.

HALTER: A simple form of headgear often made of rope, for leading and tying up.

HAYLAGE: Grass that has been cut and baled into sealed bags when partly dry.

HEADCOLLAR: Headgear made up of a noseband, headpiece and throatlash. Used for leading and tying up.

KEEPERS: The small leather loops used to hold the ends of the bridle straps neatly in place.

LAME: When an ill or injured pony cannot move without feeling discomfort.

LAMINITIS: A painful disease that

makes the feet very tender – usually caused by over-feeding.

LIVERY: Paying rent for your pony's accommodation and sometimes his care too.

LOADING: Putting a horse into a horse-box or trailer.

LOOSE BOX: An individual stable where a horse can be left loose.

LOOSE RING: A kind of joint on a bit where the rings are not fixed to the mouthpiece but can slip through it.

MANGER: A trough in a stable used for feeding.

MARTINGALE: A neckstrap attached between the forelegs to the girth and also the reins or noseband to give the rider more control.

NEAR SIDE: The pony's left-hand side.

NEW ZEALAND RUG: A tough rug for using outdoors.

NUMNAH: A cotton or fleece shaped pad used under the saddle to ease pressure and absorb sweat.

OFF-SIDE: The pony's right-hand side.

OVER-REACH: A kind of 'interference' where the pony strikes into the heels of a fore leg with the toe of one of his hind feet.

PICKING OUT: Cleaning out the hooves.

PULLING: Thinning out a thick mane or tail by taking out just a few hairs at a time.

QUARTERING: A quick groom to tidy up a pony.

ROLLED: TOE: A type of shoe used on a pony which tends to drag its feet. The metal is turned up over the toe area, protecting it.

ROLLER: A wide strap used around the belly to keep a rug in place.

SADDLE HORSE: A frame used to sit the saddle on for storage or cleaning.

SETTING FAIR: The traditional term for getting a pony and stable clean and tidy.

SKIPPING OUT: A quick 'muck-out' during the day, using a basket 'skip' to collect any droppings.

SNAFFLE: The largest and most commonly-seen family of bits, usually with one ring either side of the mouthpiece.

SOUND: A healthy horse with no breathing or lameness problems.

STALE: To urinate.

STARING COAT: A coat that is dull and sometimes standing up, indicating ill health.

STRAPPING: A thorough groom for a stable-kept horse or pony.

STUD: 1) A yard where horses are bred 2) A metal plug that can be screwed into a hole in a horseshoe, or fixed permanently, to give the horse extra grip.

SURCINGLE: A narrow strap used around the belly to fasten a rug or over the saddle for extra security when galloping and jumping.

TENDONS: Tough tissue that connects muscles to bones. In horses, the main tendons run down the back of the cannon bones in the lower legs.

TREE: The frame around which the saddle is built.

TROTTING UP: Running up and down leading a pony so someone can watch its movement.

TUCKED UP: A pony that is standing hunched and miserable, with pinched-in quarters, indicating ill health.

TURNING OUT: Letting a pony loose into a field.

UNSOUND: A pony that is lame.

VICE: A bad or nervous habit.

WEAVING: A stable 'vice' caused by boredom or frustration, where the horse rocks its head and neck from side to side repetitively.

WIND: A horse's breathing.

WORMS: Internal parasites carried by all horses. Infestation can make a pony very ill unless controlled by regular doses of 'wormer'.

Look after your pony, and he will look after you!